SUBLIME

40oz. to freedom

**Authentic
GUITAR-TAB
Edition** ™
Includes Complete Solos

This publication is not
for sale in the EU

D1270673

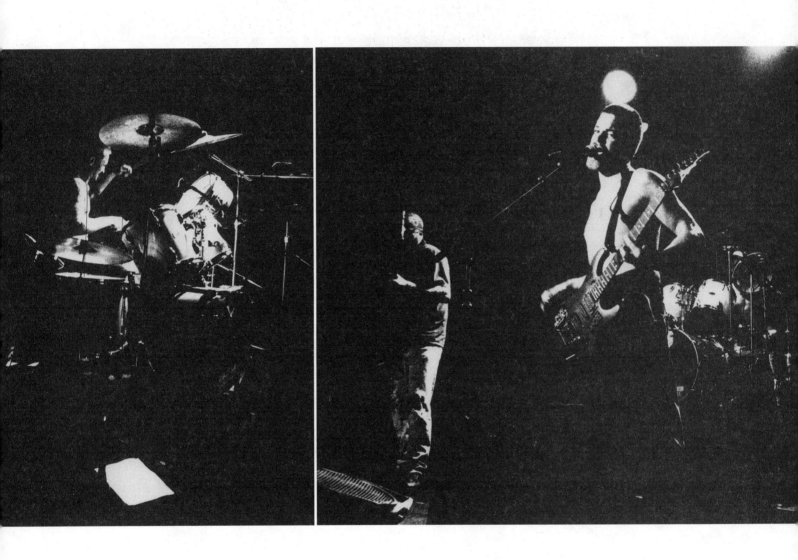

SUBLIME

40oz. to freedom

Waiting for My Ruca

Words and Music by Brad Nowell

MCA Music Publishing

love,   she send a mes-sage of   love.   She said, I

Bridge

love up the way you move, I love the   way you rap, BOPP BOPP.   Ra-mo-na, please step

Chorus

back.   'Cause she's my ru-   ca,   I'm bare-ly wait-ing for my

(Mmm. __)

Interlude

(tape effects)

hi   na.

(Vamp   up.)

(Bye, _ bye, bye, _ bye, bye. _)   3. She moved from Long Beach down to

Verse

L.   A.   Right now she's sel-ling or-an-ges by the free - way.

I wan-na know,   Ra-mo-na, am I the on-ly one? Tell me. And she said,

"You're not the on-ly one, but you're the best Brad-ly" BOOM BOOM.   And now I'm wait-ing for my

Chorus

ru-   ca and I bare-ly pulled up with my hi - na.

I know to-night I be be-hind ___ her,   don't fuck a-round _ with my hi - na.

40 Oz. to Freedom

Words and Music by Brad Nowell

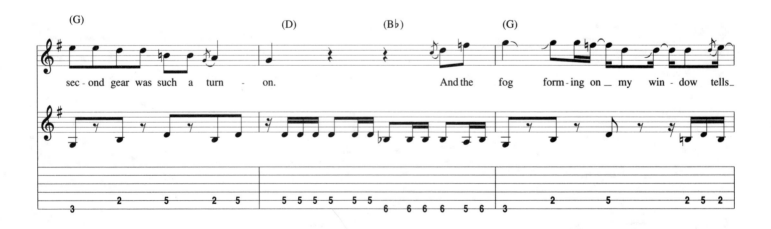

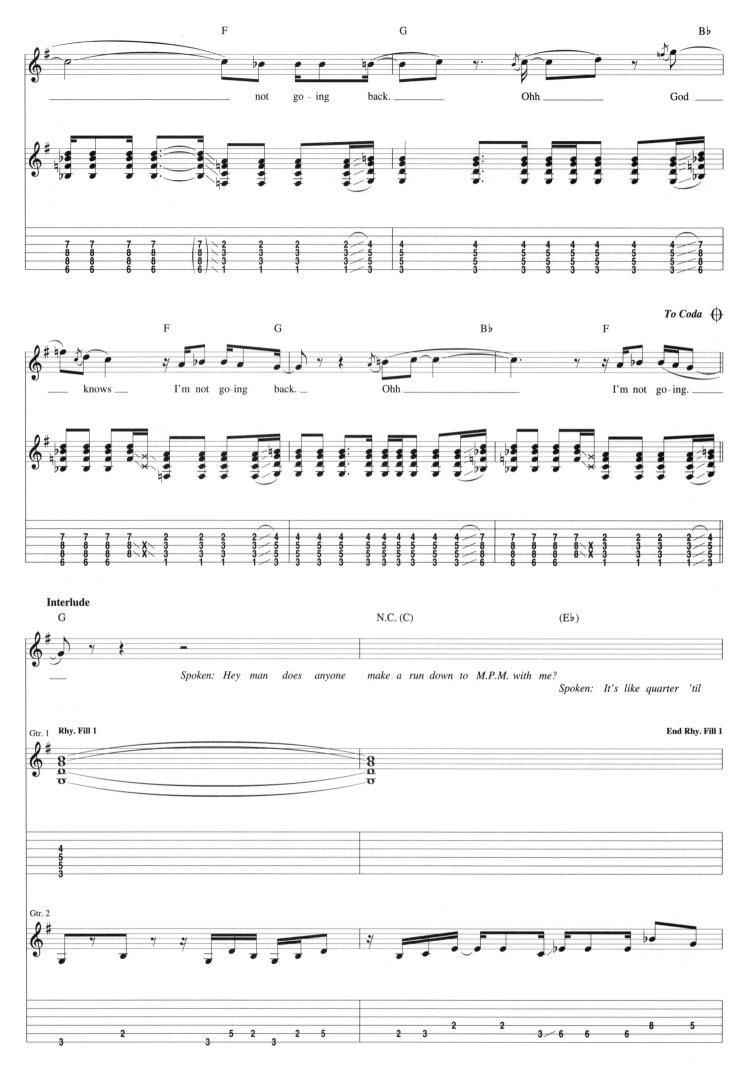

Chorus

Gtrs. 2, 3 & 4 tacet

Ohhhh... _____
(Back,   back.)

I'm _____ not go-ing back.

Gtr. 1

let ring -

Smoke Two Joints

Written by Chris Kay and Michael Kay

Intro
Free Time

(approx. 18 sec.)

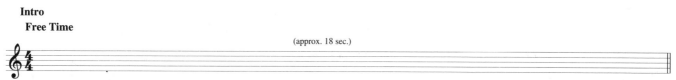

Spoken: She was living in a single room with three other individuals. One of them was a male, and the other two? Well, the other two were females. God only knows what they were up to in there. And furthermore, Susan, I wouldn't be the least bit surprised to learn that all four of them habitually smoked marijuana cigarettes. Reefers!

Verse

1. I smoke two joints_ in the morn-ing. I smoke two joints_ at night. I

Gtr. 1: w/ Rhy. Fig. 1, 3 times, simile

smoke two joints_ in the af-ter-noon. It makes me feel _ al-right. I smoke two joints _ in time of peace _ and

two in time_ of war._ I smoke two joints_ be-fore I smoke two joints,_ and then I smoke_ two more.

Interlude

pitch: G C#

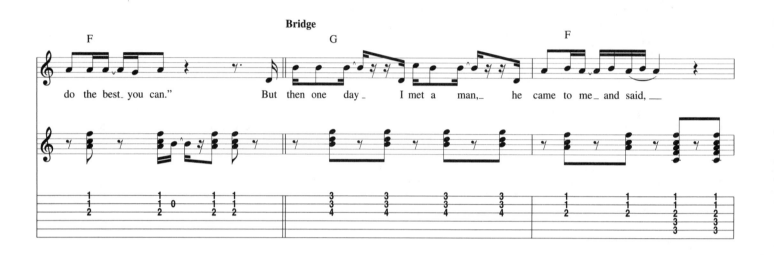

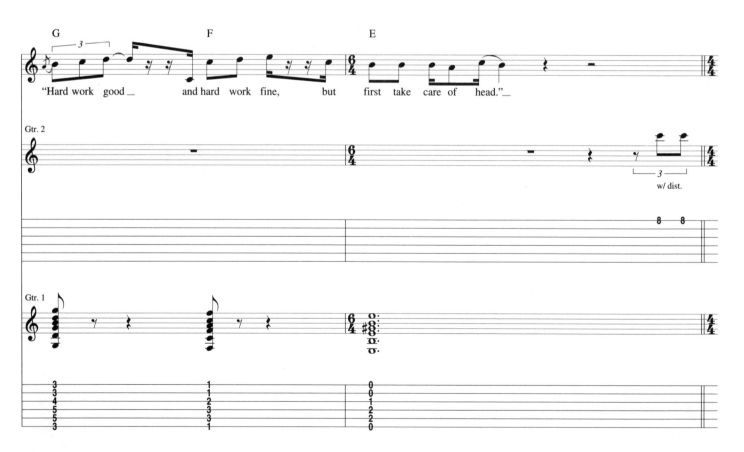

Guitar Solo

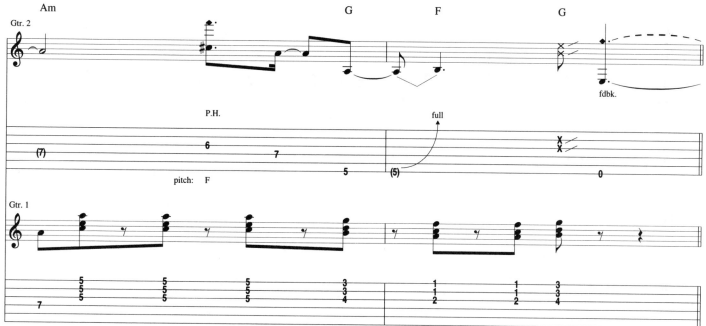

Interlude

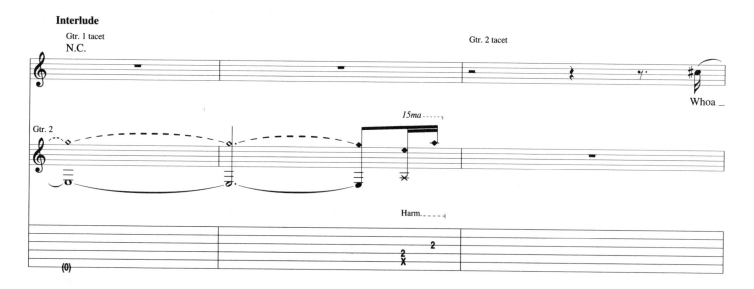

rock me   to the night. ___ Whoa, ___ Ja   say. ___

Whoa. _____

Outro
Faster ♩ = 188
Double-Time

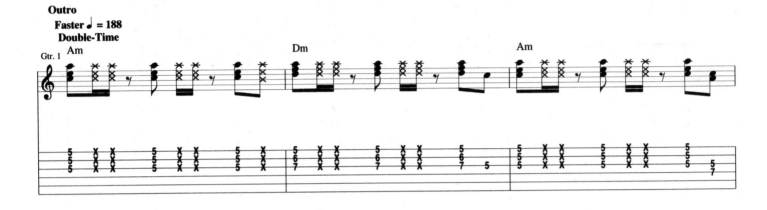

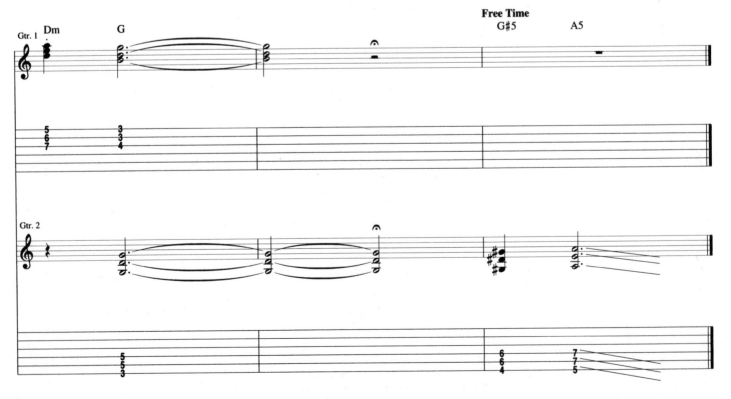

We're Only Gonna Die for Our Arrogance

Words and Music by Greg Graffin

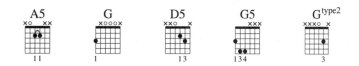

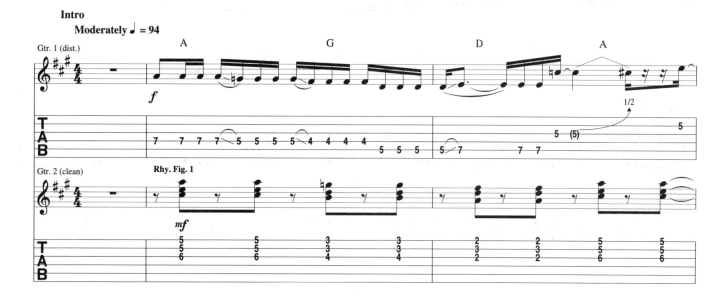

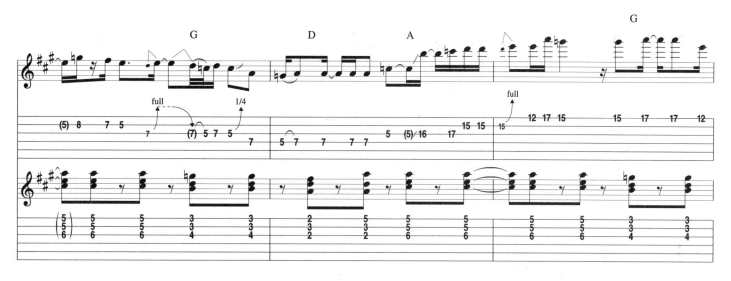

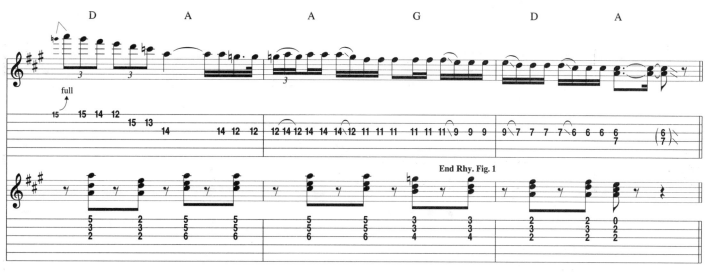

Verse

Gtr. 2: w/ Rhy. Fig. 1, simile
Gtr. 1 tacet

1. Ear-ly man walked a-way_ as mod-ern-man_ took con-trol. Their mind's weren't all_ the same;_ to__

con-quer was their goal._ So __ he built his great em-pire_ and he slaught-ered his own kind._

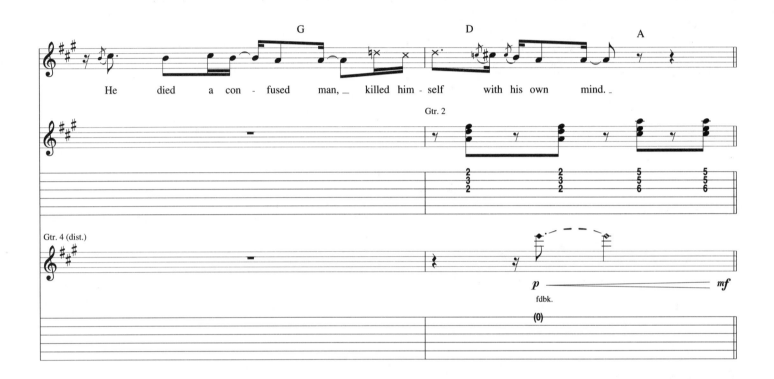

He died a con-fused man,_ killed him-self with his own mind._

Gtr. 2

Gtr. 4 (dist.)

p ———————— *mf*
fdbk.

Guitar Solo

Double-Time ♩ = 184

Gtr. 2 tacet

Gtr. 3
(dist.)

Gtr. 1

Gtr. 4 **Rhy. Fig. 2**

End Rhy. Fig. 2

P.M. - - - - - - - - - - - - - - - -   *sim.*

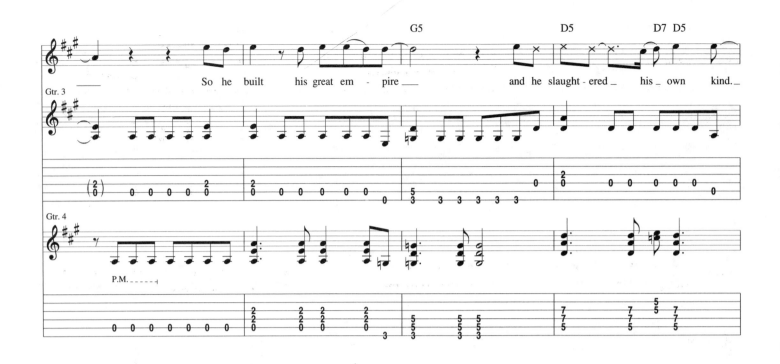

So he built his great em - pire ___ and he slaught - ered ___ his ___ own ___ kind. ___

And he died a con - fused man ___ and he killed him - self with his own mind. ___ Let's _ go!

Interlude
Faster ♩ = 204

Verse

Gtr. 1 tacet
play 4 times

3. Ear - ly man walked a - way as

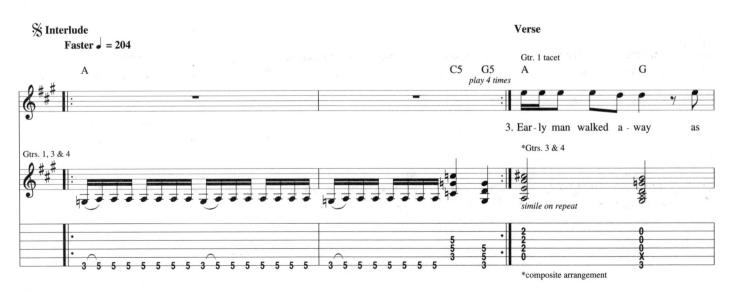

22

died a con - fused man ___ and killed him - self with his own mind. ___ Let's go!

✛ *Coda*

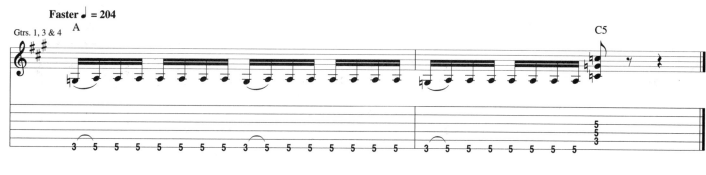

We're on - ly gon - na die ___ for

our own ar - ro - gance, ___ that's why we might as well take our time. ___

Don't Push

Words and Music by Brad Nowell

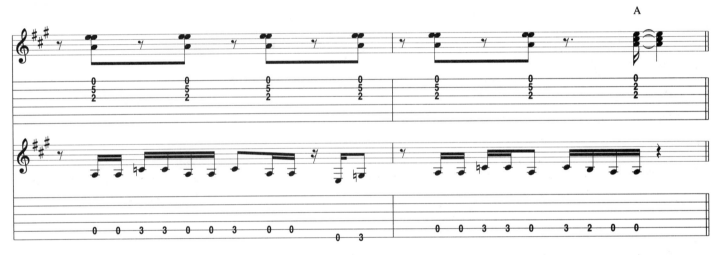

1. Stol- en from an Af - ri-can land._ Chased out with a knife._ With a face like Bob Mar - ley and a mouth_

MCA Music Publishing

was Mike Ty - son I would look for a fight. And if I was a Boom - town Rat I would be stay - in up all night. If I

let ring

was the king Ad-Rock I would get stu - pid dumb. And if rhymes __ were val - i - ums I'd be comf - 'ta - 'bly numb.

Gtr. 2 tacet

End Rhy. Fig. 2A

End Rhy. Fig. 2

Verse

2. If I ___ had a shot - gun, you know what I'd do? __ I'd point that shit straight at the sky __ and shoot

Gtr. 1

28

heav-en on down for you.___ Be-cause the bars are al-ways o-pen, and the

time is al-ways right.___ And if God's good word goes un-spo-ken, well the mu-sic goes all night. And it goes...

Bridge

Gtrs. 1 & 2: w/ Rhy. Figs. 2 & 2A, simile

I want a lov-er but I can't find the time. I want a rea-son but I can't find the rhyme and I

want to start some sta-tic but I can't af-ford. ___ Just land on the ground like I fall off my skate-board, hey.

And now-a-days ___ as clear as you please, you strap with pro-tec-tion, or strap with dis-ease. Laugh-ter, it's free

an-y time just call me Four - three - nine - o - one - one - six. When your down with Sub - lime you get

Guitar Solo

A5

fun - ky fresh lyr - ics. Mmm you get noth -

(Lyr - ics.)

Gtr. 2

Gtr. 1

Gtr. 3 (dist.)

in'.

(Yeah.)

15ma loco

8va loco

T.H.   P.H.

Verse

Gtr. 1: w/ Rhy. Fig. 1, 1st 5 meas., simile

Gtr. 2 tacet

A

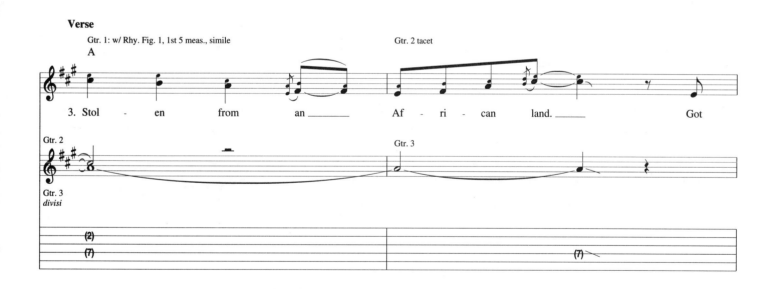

3. Stol - en   from   an ____   Af - ri - can   land. ____   Got

Gtr. 2

Gtr. 3

Gtr. 3
divisi

Gtr. 3 tacet

D   A   G   F5

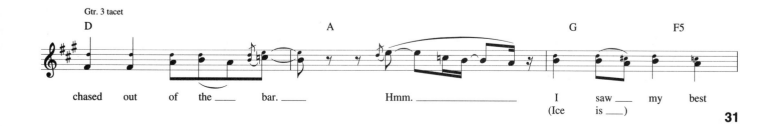

chased   out   of   the ___   bar. ___   Hmm. _____   I   saw ___   my   best
(Ice   is ___)

friend to-night so don't push me too __ far. ____

Gtr. 1

Interlude

C5   Bb5   C5   Bb5   C5   Bb5   C5

4. I'm gon-na

Rhy. Fig. 3

End Rhy. Fig. 3

Verse

Gtr. 1: w/ Rhy. Fig. 3, simile

C5   Bb5   C5   Bb5

run come down with the new lyr-ics, __ get hit, __ get hip, __ don't slip __ you knuck-le-heads. Ra-

C5   Bb5   C5

ci-sm is schi-sm on a ser-i-ous tip. __ You don't be-lieve me then I go out and bust your lip, huh.

Gtr. 1 tacet
N.C.

3

I hear the moun-tain, it hard to climb. __ Rough-er the rhy-thm, then it must be sub-lime. __

Lis-ten yel-low lov-er you got it right on time. We got crick-et with the quick-ness and the bass-line.

32

5446 That's My Number

Words and Music by Frederick Hibbert

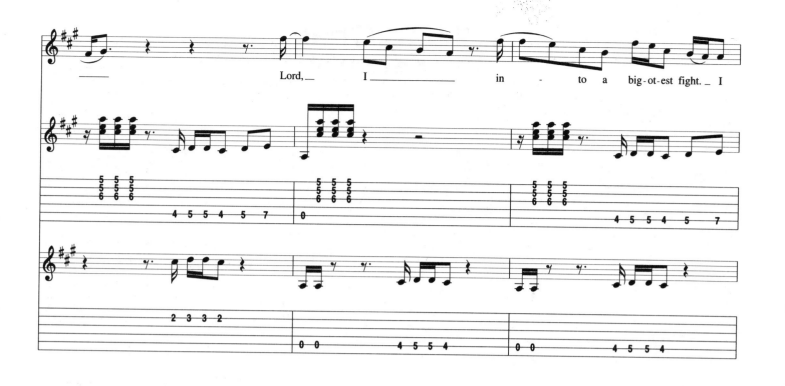

Lord, __ I _____ in - to a big-ot-est fight. _ I

wound ____ up in hell ____ all night. Mm, _ a - give it to me

Bridge

Gtr. 1: w/ Rhy. Fig. 2

Gtr. 2 tacet

A   D

one time, __   Give it to me,   two times,,, _   Give it to me,
            (Oh, yes, oh,   my pussy.)

Segue into "Ball and Chain"

three times,,, _   Give it to me,   four times,,,, _

Ball and Chain

Words and Music by Brad Nowell

months lat-ter sweet ba-bys on the way. Kiss 'em on the cheek and lifes o. k. I don't feel, no pain. I don't

have, no time to lis-ten to con-flict-ing points of view. Oh, It's a cra-

-zy world to live a-lone, a

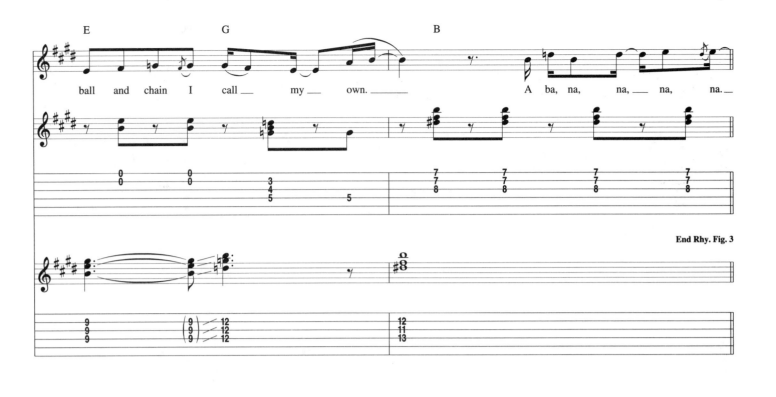

ball and chain I call ___ my ___ own. _____ A ba, na, na, ___ na, na. ___

End Rhy. Fig. 3

Interlude

Gtrs. 1 & 2: w/ Rhy. Fig. 1, 2 times, simile

E   G   E   G   E   G   E   G

___ Whoo.   Bo.

Verse

Gtr. 1: w/ Rhy. Fig. 2, simile

E   B

2. Peo-ple lis-ten up don't stand too close. ___ I've ___ got some-thing that you ___ all should know. Ho-ly Mat-ri-mo-ny's not for me.

Gtr. 2

E   B

Rath-er die a-lone in ___ mis-er-y. ___ Be-cause I ___ was al-ways taught that boy meets girl, ___ fall in love get mar-ried and for-get the world. Nine

Bridge

Gtr. 2: w/ Fill 1

months lat-er, the sweet ba-by's on the way. Is-n't that a-what they used to say? With a girl that you knew, and the

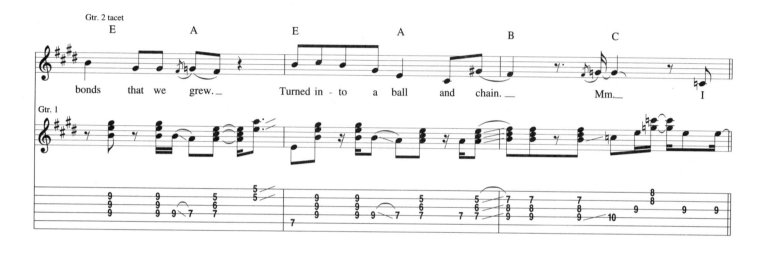

Gtr. 2 tacet

bonds that we grew.___ Turned in-to a ball and chain.___ Mm.___ I

Chorus

Gtr. 2: w/ Rhy. Fig. 3, simile

step in-to the great un-known.___ On a ball ___ and chain I call ___ my own. ___ A ba, na, na,___ na, na,

Fill 1

Gtr. 2

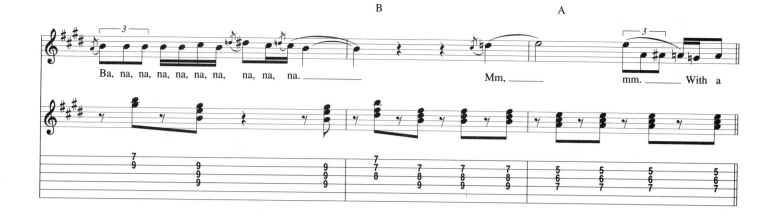

Bridge

Chorus
Double-Time ♩ = 186

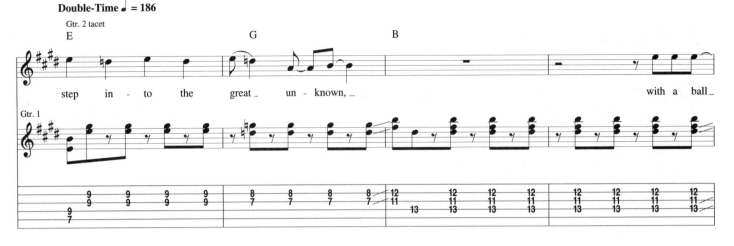

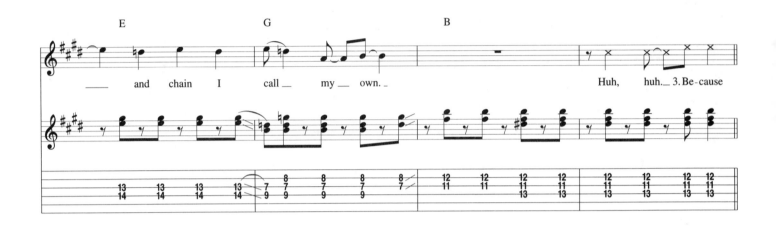

Verse

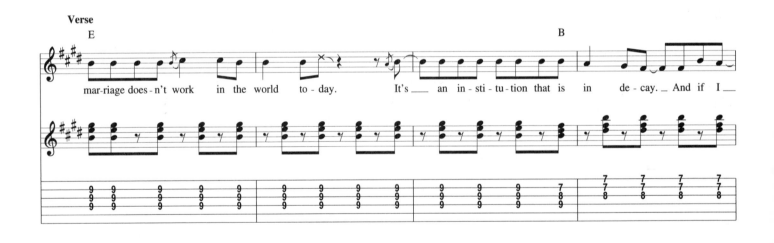

Bridge

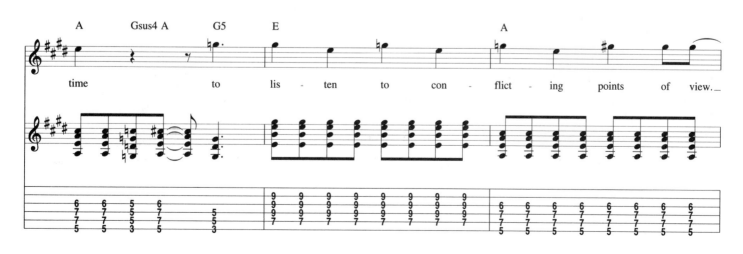

Badfish

Words and Music by Brad Nowell

Verse
Faster ♩ = 92
Gtrs. 1 & 2 tacet

1. When you grab a hold of me. ___ You tell me that I'll nev-er be ___ set free.

Rhy. Fig. 1
Gtr. 3 (elec.)
mp
w/ clean tone

But I'm a par-a-site, _____ creep and crawl I step in-to ___ the night.

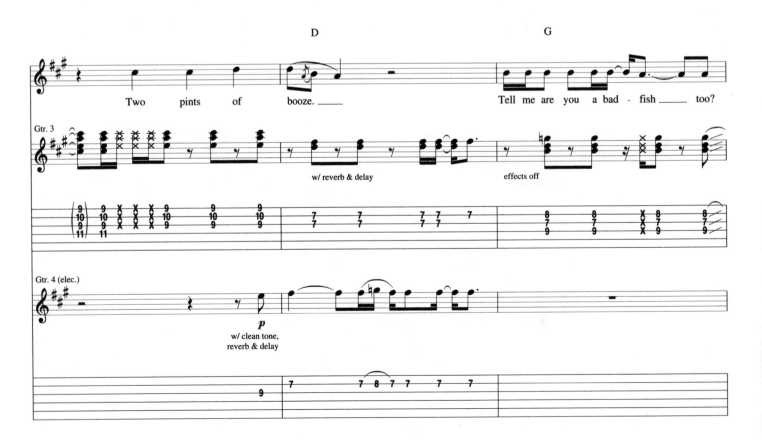

Two pints of booze. _____ Tell me are you a bad-fish ____ too?

Gtr. 3
w/ reverb & delay   effects off

Gtr. 4 (elec.)
p
w/ clean tone,
reverb & delay

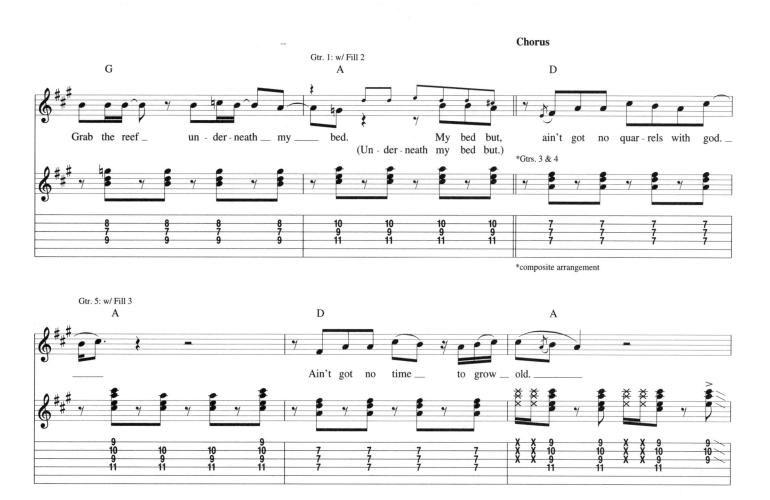

Grab the reef __ un - der - neath __ my __ bed. My bed but, ain't got no quar - rels with god. __
(Un - der - neath my bed but.)

*Gtrs. 3 & 4

*composite arrangement

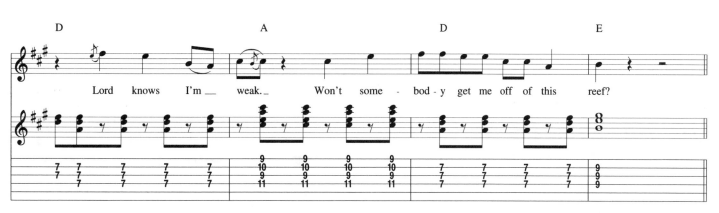

__ Ain't got no time __ to grow __ old. _____

Lord knows I'm __ weak. __ Won't some - bod - y get me off of this __ reef?

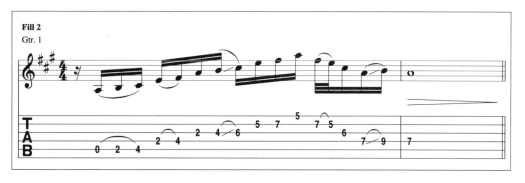

Fill 2
Gtr. 1

Fill 3
Gtr. 5 (elec.)

mf
w/ clean tone & reverse echo

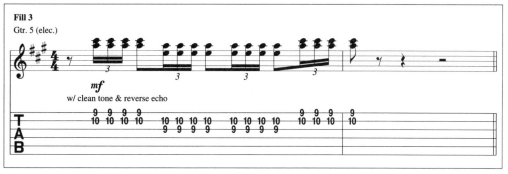

Interlude

*Played ahead of the beat.

Guitar Solo

Let's Go Get Stoned

Words and Music by Brad Nowell

New Thrash

Words and Music by Brad Nowell

tease me and try to say that I should care. I might as well go out for mine 'cause

Guitar Solo
Half-Time ♩ = 74

ev - 'ry - bod - y's go - ing out _____ for theirs. ____

pitch: G A   A   G A   F   G   F   G

Verse

A Tempo

Gtrs. 1 & 2: w/ Rhy. Fig. 1, simile

D5   A5   F5   G5

2. So don't tell me ___ a - bout a fake drug war. (Go) cut ed - u - ca - tion pro - grams more. ___ The

D5   F5   G5   *On Cue:*

Drum Solo

peo - ple ___ will one day learn and rise ___ 'cause not ev - 'ry-one is out to score.

Gtrs. 1 & 2

Verse

Gtrs. 1 & 2: w/ Rhy. Fig. 1, 1st 3 meas., simile

D5   A5   F5

3. Peo - ple al - ways ask me why peo - ple all ___ fucked up at ev - 'ry cor - ner liq - uor store. ___

G5   *On Cue:*

(drums)

Peace.

Gtrs. 1 & 2

Scarlet Begonias

Words by Robert Hunter
Music by Jerry Garcia

once in a while _ you get shown _ in the light _ in the strang - est of pla - ces if you look at it right.

Guitar Solo

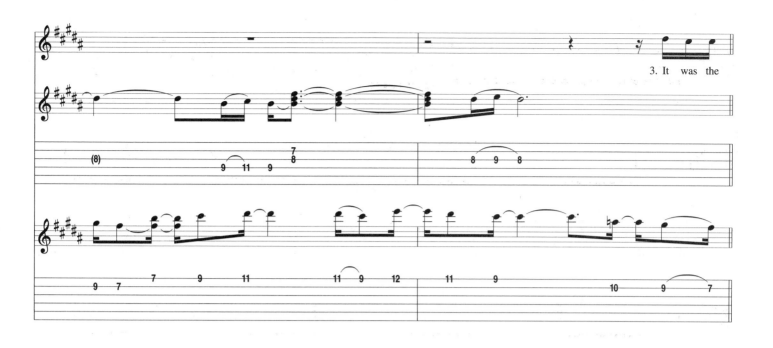

3. It was the

Verse

Gtr. 1: w/ Rhy. Fig. 2, simile
Gtr. 2: w/ Riff B, simile

sum-mer of love __ and I thank the stars a-bove be-cause the wo-man took her lov-in' o-ver me. And

Gtr. 2

just to gain her trust, I bought a mi-cro-bus be-cause I sold off all my per-son-al prop-er-ty. _____ A tie,

Bridge

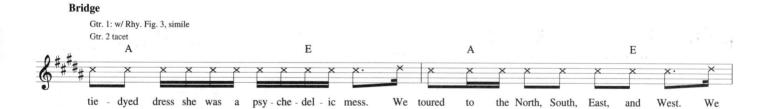

Gtr. 1: w/ Rhy. Fig. 3, simile
Gtr. 2 tacet

tie - dyed dress she was a psy-che-del-ic mess. We toured to the North, South, East, and West. We

sold some mush-room tea. We sold some ec-sta-sy. We sold ni-trous, o-pi-um, ac-id, her-o-in, and P C P. and now I

Gtr. 1: w/ Rhy. Fig. 1, simile
Gtr. 2: w/ Riff A, simile

hear the po-lice com-ing af-ter __ me. _____ Yes now I hear the po-lice com-ing af-ter me. The

one scar-let with the flow-ers in her hair, she's got the po-lice com-ing __ af-ter me. Well there ain't__

⊕ Coda

by. Oh, just to let her pass __ by.

Outro

Begin Fade ... **Fade Out**

Live at E's

Words and Music by Brad Nowell

Interlude

Gtr. 1: w/ Rhy. Fig. 1, 4 times, simile
Gtr. 2 tacet

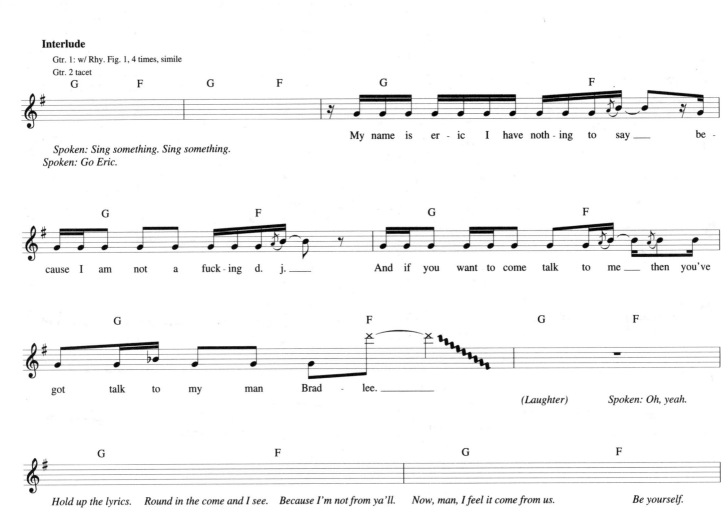

Spoken: *Sing something. Sing something.*
Spoken: *Go Eric.*

My name is er - ic I have noth - ing to say ___ be -

cause I am not a fuck - ing d. j. ___ And if you want to come talk to me ___ then you've

got talk to my man Brad - lee. ___ (*Laughter*) Spoken: *Oh, yeah.*

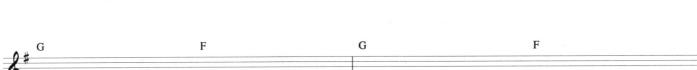

Hold up the lyrics. Round in the come and I see. Because I'm not from ya'll. Now, man, I feel it come from us. Be yourself.

So if my lyrics are for your fuck, comb it, for it, for my lone man. See. That's why ya'll come to see it. My rock, it

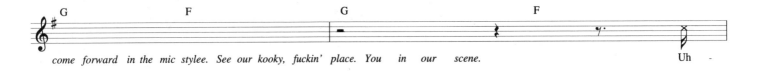

come forward in the mic stylee. See our kooky, fuckin' place. You in our scene. Uh -

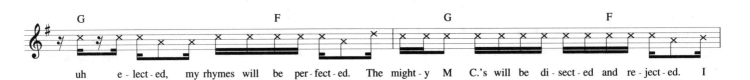

uh e - lect - ed, my rhymes will be per - fect - ed. The might - y M C.'s will be di - sect - ed and re - ject - ed. I

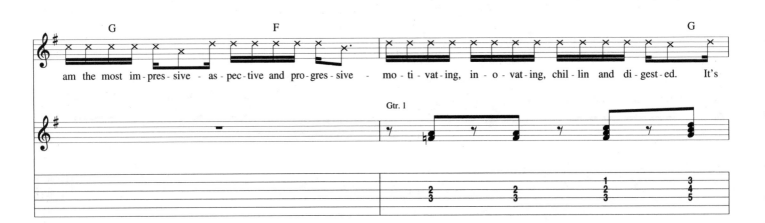

am the most im - pres - sive - as - pec - tive and pro - gres - sive - mo - ti - vat - ing, in - o - vat - ing, chil - lin and di - gest - ed. It's

D.J.s

Words and Music by Brad Nowell

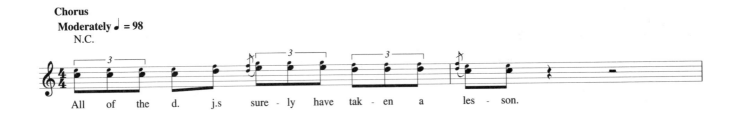

Bridge

___ ain't noth-in wrong, ___ ain't noth-ing right ___ and still I set and lie a-wake all night. ___

Chorus

Gtr. 1: w/ Rhy. Fig. 1, 2 times, simile

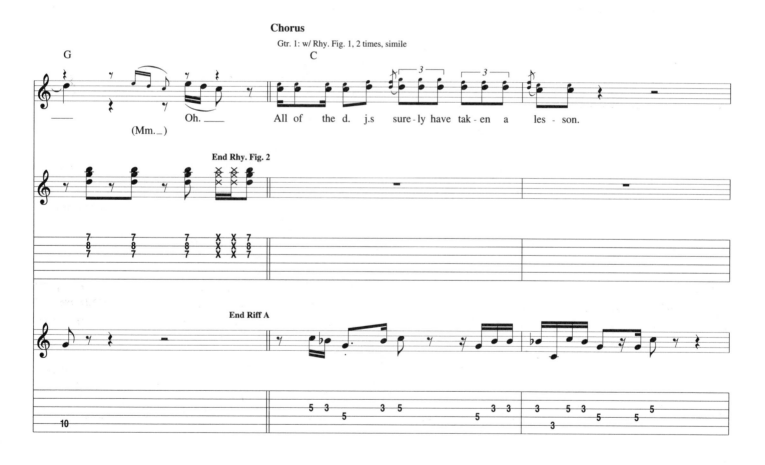

___ Oh. ___ All of the d. j.s sure-ly have tak-en a les-son.

(Mm. ___)

Try talk-in' trash and I'll come with my Smith and Wes-son. 2. E -

Outro

Gtrs. 1 & 2 tacet
N.C.

I won't wait so long. Mm. I said I won't

wait so long for you. Oh, oh, yeah. Mm,

mm. Oo, oh. Hard to get so

nn-not. Mm, mm. Stop your mes-sin' a-round. Ah.

Bet-ter think of your fu-ture. Ah.

Time to straight-en right out. Ah. Or you'll wind up in jail.

Chica Me Tipo

Words and Music by Brad Nowell

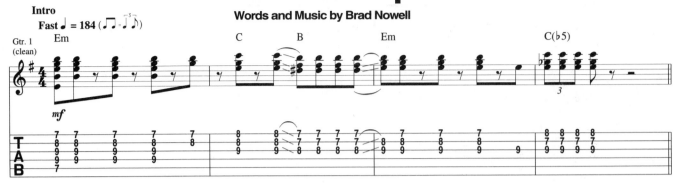

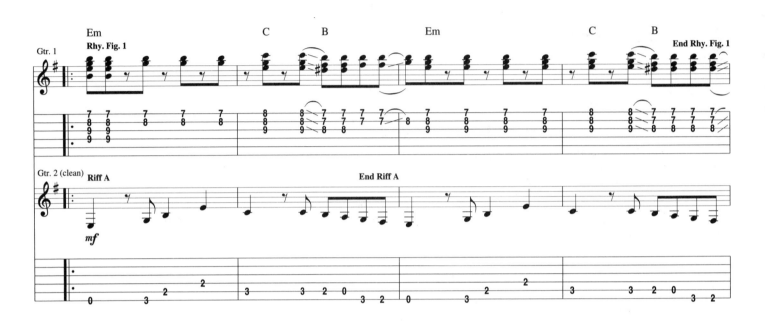

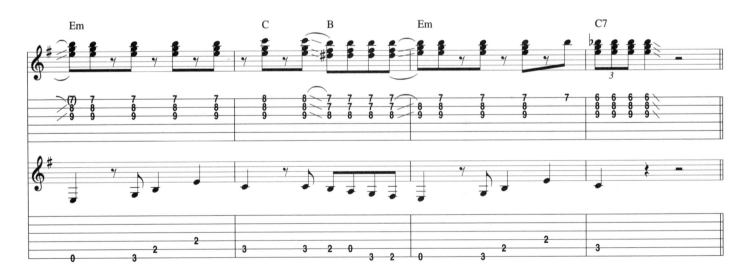

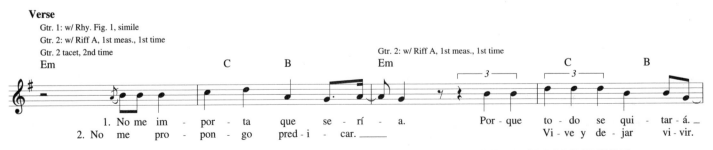

1. No me im - por - ta que se - rí - a. Por - que to - do se qui - tar - á.
2. No me pro - pon - go pred - i - car. Vi - ve y de - jar vi - vir.

Right Back

Words and Music by Brad Nowell

MCA Music Publishing

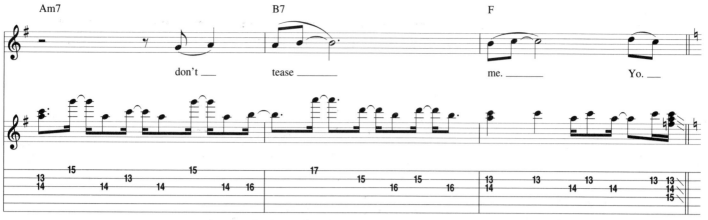

What Happened

Words and Music by Brad Nowell

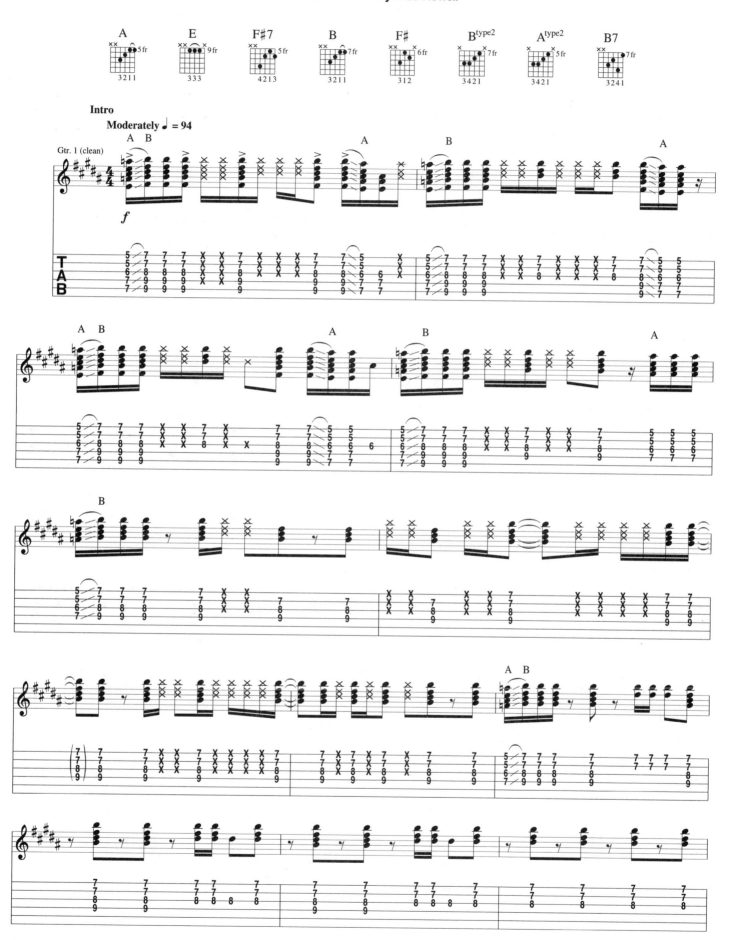

New Song

Words and Music by Brad Nowell

MCA Music Publishing

Ebin

Words and Music by Brad Nowell

Spoken: *"You can hear the fuckin' fleas crawlin' on my nuts."*

Out my win-dow cool and bright. Fade so slow-ly in-to night.

Fun-ny how things look the same now that my friend Eb-in's changed.

MCA Music Publishing

Verse

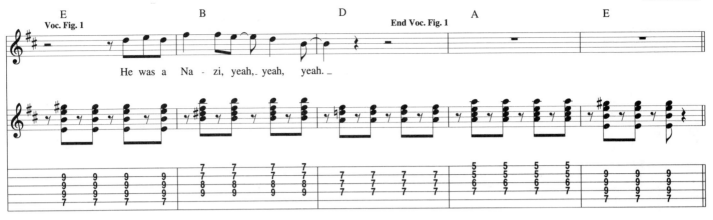

Bridge
Bm
D
A
Oh, you changed.
Eadd13
Chorus
Bm
Oh, how you changed.
I give you a hard time,
did-n't want to stay
To Coda
D
A
Got out-ta-jail just the ver-y next day.
It's plain to see
Interlude
E
B
D
A
my friend Eb-in is a Na-zi.

He was a Na - zi, yeah, yeah, yeah.

Coda

My friend Eb - in is a Na - zi.

Gtr. 1

Gtr. 2

Guitar Solo

Gtr. 3 (dist.)

Gtr. 1

*Microphonic fdbk, not caused by string vibration.

Date Rape

Words and Music by Brad Nowell

Intro
Moderately Fast ♩ = 172

N.C. (E)

(A)

Riff A

*Gtr. 1

mf
w/ fingers

*Horns arr. for gtr.

Verse

Gtr. 1 tacet

2.
Faster ♩ =194

G   F#   F   Em

1. Let me tell you a-bout a girl I know, ___ had a drink a-bout an

Gtr. 2 (clean)

Rhy. Fig. 1

mp   *mf*

Gtr. 1

End Riff A

Am

B   C   B

hour a-go. ___ Sit-ting in the cor-ner ___ by her-self, ___ in a bar, in down-town Hell.

Gtr. 2

End Rhy. Fig. 1

Gtr. 2: w/ Rhy. Fig. 1, simile

Em

She heard a noise   and she looked through the door. ___   And saw a man she'd nev-er   seen be-fore. ___

Am

B   C   B

Light skin,   light blue eyes, ___   a dou-ble chin and a plas-tic smile. ___ Well,

MCA Music Publishing

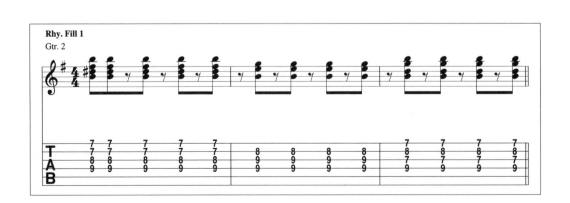

Hope

Written by Milo Auckerman

KRS - One

Words and Music by Brad Nowell and Lawrence Parker
Contains sample of "The Style You Haven't Done" and "You Must Learn" by Lawrence Parker

MCA Music Publishing

Guitar Notation Legend

Guitar Music can be notated three different ways: on a *musical staff*, in *tablature*, and in *rhythm slashes*.

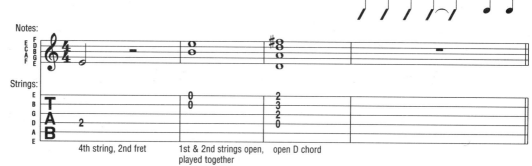

RHYTHM SLASHES are written above the staff. Strum chords in the rhythm indicated. Use the chord diagrams found at the top of the first page of the transcription for the appropriate chord voicings. Round noteheads indicate single notes.

THE MUSICAL STAFF shows pitches and rhythms and is divided by bar lines into measures. Pitches are named after the first seven letters of the alphabet.

TABLATURE graphically represents the guitar fingerboard. Each horizontal line represents a string, and each number represents a fret.

4th string, 2nd fret / 1st & 2nd strings open, played together / open D chord

HALF-STEP BEND: Strike the note and bend up 1/2 step.

WHOLE-STEP BEND: Strike the note and bend up one step.

GRACE NOTE BEND: Strike the note and bend up as indicated. The first note does not take up any time.

SLIGHT (MICROTONE) BEND: Strike the note and bend up 1/4 step.

BEND AND RELEASE: Strike the note and bend up as indicated, then release back to the original note. Only the first note is struck.

PRE-BEND: Bend the note as indicated, then strike it.

VIBRATO: The string is vibrated by rapidly bending and releasing the note with the fretting hand.

WIDE VIBRATO: The pitch is varied to a greater degree by vibrating with the fretting hand.

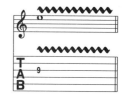

HAMMER-ON: Strike the first (lower) note with one finger, then sound the higher note (on the same string) with another finger by fretting it without picking.

PULL-OFF: Place both fingers on the notes to be sounded. Strike the first note and without picking, pull the finger off to sound the second (lower) note.

LEGATO SLIDE: Strike the first note and then slide the same fret-hand finger up or down to the second note. The second note is not struck.

SHIFT SLIDE: Same as legato slide, except the second note is struck.

TRILL: Very rapidly alternate between the notes indicated by continuously hammering on and pulling off.

TAPPING: Hammer ("tap") the fret indicated with the pick-hand index or middle finger and pull off to the note fretted by the fret hand.

NATURAL HARMONIC: Strike the note while the fret-hand lightly touches the string directly over the fret indicated.

PINCH HARMONIC: The note is fretted normally and a harmonic is produced by adding the edge of the thumb or the tip of the index finger of the pick hand to the normal pick attack.

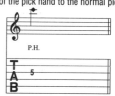

PICK SCRAPE: The edge of the pick is rubbed down (or up) the string, producing a scratchy sound.

MUFFLED STRINGS: A percussive sound is produced by laying the fret hand across the string(s) without depressing, and striking them with the pick hand.

PALM MUTING: The note is partially muted by the pick hand lightly touching the string(s) just before the bridge.

RAKE: Drag the pick across the strings indicated with a single motion.

TREMOLO PICKING: The note is picked as rapidly and continuously as possible.

VIBRATO BAR DIVE AND RETURN: The pitch of the note or chord is dropped a specified number of steps (in rhythm) then returned to the original pitch.

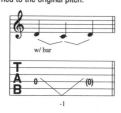

VIBRATO BAR SCOOP: Depress the bar just before striking the note, then quickly release the bar.

VIBRATO BAR DIP: Strike the note and then immediately drop a specified number of steps, then release back to the original pitch.